FAULT

THREE PLAYS BY
NICOLAS BILLON

LINES

GREENLAND | ICELAND | FAROE ISLANDS

COACH HOUSE BOOKS | TORONTO

Canada Council   Conseil des Arts
for the Arts   du Canada    ONTARIO ARTS COUNCIL
CONSEIL DES ARTS DE L'ONTARIO   Canadä

Published with the generous assistance of the Canada Council for the Arts
and the Ontario Arts Council. Coach House Books also gratefully
acknowledges the support of the Government of Canada through the
Canada Book Fund and the Government of Ontario through the Ontario
Book Publishing Tax Credit.

LIBRARY AND ARCHIVES CANADA CATALOGUING IN PUBLICATION

Billon, Nicolas
        Fault lines : three plays / by Nicolas Billon.

Contents: Greenland -- Iceland -- Faroe Islands.
Issued also in electronic format.
ISBN 978 1 55245 276 9

I. Billon, Nicolas Greenland. 2. Billon, Nicolas Iceland. 3. Billon,
Nicolas Faroe Islands. 4. Title. 5. Title: Plays. Selections.

PS8603.I44A62013   C842'.6   C2013-900311-8

Fault Lines is dedicated to three of my favourite collaborators:

Greenland
　　　　is for Claire Calnan

Iceland
　　　　is for Ravi Jain

Faroe Islands
　　　　is for Kat Chin

PLAYWRIGHT'S NOTE

The only advice I have for staging these plays is this: strive for simplicity.

Director Ravi Jain and I discovered this when working on *Greenland*. Throughout the rehearsal process, we whittled everything (text, acting, design, direction) down to the essential. It was terrifying. And it worked.

There is no spectacle to speak of; there is only the narrative which the actor must illuminate in the heart of each audience member. To use a film metaphor, these plays are meant to be shot in close-up. Or perhaps a better image is that of a confessional?

In any case, the goal is the same: to connect.

I hope you enjoy them and, especially, that you find something that resonates with you.

Nicolas Billon
February 2013

GREENLAND

GREENLAND

Greenland premiered at the SummerWorks Theatre Festival on August 7, 2009, with the following artistic team:

Jonathan: Andrew Musselman
Judith: Claire Calnan
Tanya: Jajube Mandiela

Director: Ravi Jain
Production Designer: Ken MacKenzie
Stage Manager: Kat Chin
Assistant Director: Natalia Naranjo
Producer: Roxanne Duncan

Winner of the 2009 SummerWorks Prize for Outstanding Production

Greenland subsequently opened at the New York International Fringe Festival on August 12, 2011, with the following artistic team:

Jonathan: Andrew Musselman
Judith: Claire Calnan
Tanya: Susan Heyward

Director: Ravi Jain
Production Designer: Christopher D'Angelo
Stage Manager: Michelle Foster
Assistant Director: Esther Barlow
Producers: Dustin Olson and Esther Barlow

Winner of the 2011 NYC Fringe Overall Excellence Award for Playwriting

JONATHAN

Jonathan nurses a glass filled with ice and whiskey.

He swirls the ice. Looks at it. Listens to it.

So, after he cut off my baby toe, Miteq threw it in the Arctic Ocean. It was an offering to Arnakuagsak, the mercurial goddess who lives at the bottom of the sea. How'd she react to my frostbitten toe? Disgust? Perplexity? Perhaps it was rent for spending the night alone on her island, which was now, technically, my island.

We found it while collecting ice samples, about 300 kilometres north of Kulusuk.

The island was quite large, and maybe a dozen metres off the coast? I didn't remember it from any of the maps; Miteq was equally baffled by it, and we're talking about someone who can draw the outline of the coast on the palm of his hand. My hypothesis – which ended up being correct – was that it used to be connected to the mainland by the ice sheet, which is why it was mapped as part of Greenland, but that because of the glacial retreat, it was no longer 'attached' and was an island proper. And this was a big deal – the island is roughly four square kilometres, the first significant land mass discovery since the Antarctic islands in the 1800s, probably.

And it meant I could name it.

We flew in by helicopter the next day. I felt a ... an attraction? A pull towards this island. I decided to camp there overnight – a way of claiming it, perhaps? I don't know. But it's something I felt compelled to do, and do alone.

Jonathan rubs his forehead.

Now, before I tell you about ... I think it's important to mention that I had no romantic notions about Greenland. I was curious, yes, even excited to be finally going there. Perhaps because I knew it would be my last summer doing field work. (I'd promised Judith.) But I never thought, I never expected ... to ... to ... Look, I went there to do research, to collect ice samples, to ask *questions* ...

Jonathan smiles.

At my wedding, my mother joked that I was born with a silver question mark in my mouth. The story goes that the first word I spoke as a toddler was 'Why?,' and that I haven't stopped since. She got the requisite laughs, and I remember grinning sheepishly at Judith. She shrugged, you know, as if to say, 'What can you do? She's right.'

I'm not gonna lie to you. That moment gave me pause. Because the thought that ran through my mind was, 'You are marrying a woman who is interested in answers.'

When I was eight – maybe I was nine – my mother got fed up with my constant why-why-why. She sat me down and told me that at some point, when I was a little older maybe, I'd realize that most questions have a single answer that must not only satisfy me but fill me with solace. The first thing I said was, 'What's solace?' Comfort and peace. The next thing I said was, 'What's the answer?' But she wouldn't tell me. 'You'll discover it on your own,' she said. 'It's a three-letter word.'

'And it's not "Dad."'

Unfortunately for my mother, 'God' wasn't the answer I came up with.

Raises his glass and shakes it.

Ice.

Jonathan smiles.

I can explain to you the reasons why ice is a fascinating material, objectively speaking, I mean, many of its properties are unique and quite astounding, but that won't tell you what it does to me, what it makes me feel ...

Jonathan rubs his forehead.

All right. Like the time the twins asked me to describe what a mango tastes like. (They're allergic.) And the simplicity of the question belies the conundrum that it actually is, because my only point of reference is a mango. So I can only explain it tautologically: a mango tastes like a mango.

Jonathan shrugs.

Tanya and Thomas weren't impressed either.

Anyway, that's how it is with ice. It's difficult to explain it if you've never ... been there. On a glacier.

A couple of years ago, I read this book – uh, shit, I forget the title, I didn't like the rest that much ... Anyway, the opening line was about this guy who was about to be executed and the memory, the thing he remembers right before he dies, is the first time his father took him to see ice. And I couldn't get that image out of my mind. Because the earliest memory, well, the earliest complete memory of my father is also ice.

Indicates his glass.

My father's three-letter solace was rye.

After dinner, he'd move to the sofa in the TV room and watch the Habs or whatever else was on. I'd go to him, eager, a little spaniel, and I'd wait. He'd pretend not to see me – it was a game, you understand – and eventually he'd look in my direction and, feigning surprise, he'd say, 'Why don't you fix your dad a drink?' I'd run into the kitchen and I had to use a stool to reach the freezer, standing on my tippy toes, and I'd take three ice cubes and put them in a glass – just like this one, and bring it to my dad. He had the bottle ready, and he let me pour but always kept his hands on mine, to make sure I didn't spill any. And I can vividly remember the sound as the alcohol hit the ice cubes.

He called them Johnny Titanics, a reference to both the drinker – John – and its fixer ...

Points to himself.

Jonathan.

I'd hand him the drink, he'd tousle my hair, or pat my cheek, and on a few rare occasions, he'd kiss me on the forehead. And then he'd say, 'Down the hatch!' and a few years later, the Johnny Titanics caught up with him and sunk his liver.

Looks at his drink.

He would crunch the ice cubes. One by one.

So, today, whenever I open the freezer ... That sound? The *whoosh* of the door opening, the white mist, the smell ... I think of my father. Oh, and when I sneeze. We sneeze in exactly the same way.

Takes a sip from his glass. A memory resurfaces.
Jonathan chuckles.

I once explained to the twins what I did in the field, and I was telling them about boring through ice when Thomas stopped me and asked, 'What's boring?' I explained to him that as a verb it meant drilling a hole through something. And he said ... Actually, maybe it was Tanya who said this, I can't remember, one of them said, 'Is boring boring?'

Jonathan laughs.

I thought it was pretty clever for a twelve-year-old.

Anyway. Okay. So where was I?

Right, so I decided to spend the night on my island, the island I'd just discovered ... And I was boiling water to make tea, thinking about what the island meant, could mean, to our family. Here, at last, was something real, something concrete about what it is I do. That Judith would understand, maybe. Something that wasn't mired in theories and ideas.

And I thought about the twins, well, about Thomas, about how I wished he were alive to see all this ... I think he would have appreciated the ... the Christopher-Columbus-ness of it all, you know?

Jonathan smiles.

So I was thinking of Thomas ...

And that's when I heard it – a sudden, wet exhalation. I looked up and a narwhal had breached not ten metres from the shore, its tusk gleaming in the sun. I'd never seen one before.

They're called the 'unicorn of the seas,' but the etymology of their name is fascinating. 'Narwhal,' it's old Norse and it means 'corpse whale,' because it looks ashen, like a ... well, like a corpse.

Look, I know it was a coincidence that I was thinking of Thomas when it breached. Of course. But I couldn't help it: I felt it was a sign. It was ... There was ... something *profound* about it. I mean, I felt connected to this place, to the whole universe in a way I'd never experienced before. And I'm not talking about God. At least, not in a religious sense, this isn't about a conversion ... Let me rephrase. On that island, I found the idea of God, an understanding of what God *could potentially be*. That may seem strange, not only because I'm a scientist and an atheist, but also because if you wanted to argue for a country that God left behind, I think Greenland would be at the top of that list.

So, when I woke up the next morning, I found myself with a swollen foot; it was frostbitten, and I was extremely lucky that I didn't lose the whole thing.

Takes a sip from his glass.

Since word's gotten out about the island, I've been getting phone calls from journalists – lots and lots of journalists – who want to hear about the newly discovered Thomas Morrissey Island, baptized after my nephew.

The first few interviews were ... difficult.

I would start with, 'I'm a glaciologist.' And they would ask, 'What's that?'

So I'd explain: 'Well, uh, it's complicated in the sense that it's an interdisciplinary branch of science that pulls together aspects of geology, geophysics, climatology, geography, et cetera, to examine the natural phenomena of ice in general and glaciers in particular and ... '

Are you bored yet?

Jonathan smiles.

Judith once said to me, 'The only thing you're good at communicating is your passion for things no one else understands.'

Jonathan shrugs.

The next question, invariably: 'Oh. And how did you get into that line of work?'

'Ah!' I would answer, 'Well, that's an interesting story, because I initially wanted to be a physicist, you see, but I discovered that glaciers provide a kind of unified object to explain – in a simple way – many of the complex properties of physics ... '

By this time, most interviewers are ready to hang up the phone. I could tell, mostly, from their breathing and the way they'd ask questions with a kind of fatalism, that they weren't going to like the answer. They knew what I discovered was important, but they didn't understand why.

This one guy, though, from the *New York Times*, got what I was talking about; his background was in science. At the end of the interview, he said, 'Dr. Fahey, can I be straight with you? You're selling the science, not the story. And journalists want you to give them a story. Don't talk to me about glaciology in terms of geophysics and geology; I don't know what that means. Tell me you're the Ice Whisperer. And I don't care about carbon dioxide levels in the ice. I want you to tell me that ice is saying to us, to humanity, that we're royally fucked. That's a story, that's a story I can sell. I need the, the ... '

'Mythology.'

'Yes! You give me that, and your message'll get across to people.'

I confess, my first thought was, 'Americans!' But he was right. Mythology was the thing that, until then, I'd not understood. So my next interview ...

'I'm a glaciologist.'

'Can you explain to our readers what that is, Dr. Fahey?'

'Certainly. In the same way that each of us is the product of our history – where we've come from, our life experience, our social context, et cetera – ice is the product of its history. It has a story to tell, and that's my job. To figure out what ice can tell us about its past, a hundred or even a thousand years ago. Where did it come from, why is it here, how long has it been here, what's happening to it now? Ice, like us, has its own mythology, and we can learn a lot about our past from it.'

'What is the ice telling us, Dr. Fahey?'

'That we're in trouble.'

Now that's glaciology done *sexy*.

Jonathan smiles, then sniffs the air.

Do you smell that?

He realizes what it is.

The crazy thing about Greenland is that in summer, it's light twenty-four hours a day. Sleep is hard, sometimes, and one thing that started happening was that I had waking dreams ... There's one, one in particular ... It was more like a fantasy, I suppose ... I thought I'd meet a woman – Danish, perhaps, tall, not necessarily beautiful but pretty, buxom, bookish. She, too, would be a stranger to Greenland, a visitor. Perhaps she's an ethnographer, or a linguist studying Greenlandic. She'd be married, or maybe have a serious boyfriend back in Copenhagen. But she'd fall in love with the landscape, with the ice, and wouldn't want to go home. We'd talk about it – we'd commiserate – until finally we both had the courage to stay, forget our creature comforts back home and live there, on my island, and spend the evenings reading together and have children who'd sleep in our bed, raise them as Greenlanders ... She and I would grow old together, until one evening I'd return home and find her dead – peacefully, of old age – and I'd take her outside, but not to bury her, no, I'd set her there to freeze so that I could bring her back in every evening, to share a meal and read to her and pray ...

Registers his word choice.

... no, *wish* that it would be my turn soon. And when I'd feel Death nearby, I'd take my lover to the edge of the island and bind her to me – like this, like a backpack, like an air tank, and throw myself into the Arctic Ocean.

Jonathan finishes his drink. He crunches an ice cube.

I remember now. The title of that book. It was *One Hundred Years of Solitude.*

JUDITH

Judith takes a long drag on her cigarette. She savours the nicotine, then blows out the smoke.

She takes in the audience.

Fuck the polar bears.

Fuck global warming, fuck the Kyoto Protocol, fuck seals and whales and *penguins*, okay? Fuck greenhouse gases and fuck Greenland, for that matter, and fuck you if you're sitting there thinking, 'Ever heard of cancer, bitch?'

Takes a drag from her cigarette.

I don't really mean any of that. Well, except for the part about the smoking. Because if you think I don't see the contempt in your eyes, well, *actually*, it glows in the fucking dark.

Hey. Hey. I'm gonna let you in on a little secret.

We *know* it's bad for us.

Is that what drives you crazy? That we smoke even though we know it's killing us? Yeah, well, we've all eaten a doughnut and we've all had fast food and we've all had questionable unprotected sex. So let's consider before casting the first stone, okay?

Takes a long drag from her cigarette.

To answer your question: yes, I'm in a foul mood.

Stands the cigarette up on its end and presents it to the audience.

This was my wedding gift to Jonathan: that I would stop smoking. His to me was to start drinking.

She shakes her head.

17

The man wouldn't touch a drop of alcohol. God knows why. At first I thought, okay, ex-alcoholic ... but no. It didn't bother me, to each his own, you know? But there's a point when you get tired of having a boyfriend who orders *ginger ale* every time you're out. So I made him promise me to start drinking – just a little bit, you know, to *loosen up*. Alcohol, after all, is the fuel of spontaneous combustion, right?

Takes a long drag from her cigarette.

Boom.

Judith smiles.

On the plus side, having a boyfriend who doesn't drink means there's no argument about the designated driver. But. *But.* There is a significant *lack*, a significant *absence*, a significant *dearth* of something very important: drunk sex. Sure, it can work if only I'm hammered, but let's say there's a certain *abandon* that comes when both partners are drunk.

Because what would happen is, we'd come home, I'd be three sheets, my hands are practically down his pants, I am, as they say, I am *throwing* myself at him, I am *begging* him to let me *do* certain things, I am implying in no uncertain terms that he can have his way with me, and he, he takes me by the wrists and says, 'You are drunk.'

This is what I get for marrying a scientist. Such keen observations! To point something out that, clearly, must have escaped my notice ... It's a little bit like the non-smokers out there. I mean, *thank you*.

But I'm not about to be brushed off like that – okay, sure, we can play hard to get, and if I'm not exactly subtle when I'm sober, when I'm liquored up I make Louis C. K. sound like a Sunday sermon. He's all, 'Okay, let's get you to sleep,' blah di blah blah blah. I say, 'Fuck! Me!' because I am not letting him off the hook, I am working my magic ...

Wiggles her fingers.

... and finally he relents, 'Okay, okay!' and he takes me up to the *bedroom* ...

Judith rolls her eyes.

... and I can't get my clothes off fast enough, he's fucking *folding* his laundry, whatever, we get into bed and he ...

She laughs.

He ... he goes *down* on me.
   Now normally, I wouldn't object, but COME THE FUCK ON. I don't want to be *romanced*, I don't want to be *wooed*, I want to be *fucked*, okay?

Judith sighs.

I only tell this story to illustrate a point about Jonathan and me. Which I've forgotten.

Takes a long drag on her cigarette.

So this is how I punish him. My petty little revenge. He knows what I'm doing. He's got a bloodhound's sense of smell.

She takes a last drag on her cigarette then puts it out.

Okay. I feel a little bit better.
   The only time he tries, he *attempts* to communicate is to talk to me about ice. Ice. Or Greenland. Who gives a shit?

Judith shakes her head.

I am being, as my sister would say, *ungenerous* at the moment.

And I suppose, yes, there is some truth to that.

I have one memory about Greenland. My sister and I had a subscription to *National Geographic* – it was our dad's idea – and one day, I guess I was about nine and my sister was about Tanya's age, thirteen–fourteen, an issue came in and on the cover was a picture of this mummified child they'd found in Greenland. We were terrified. Neither of us would even touch the damn magazine. I had nightmares, okay? It was the creepiest thing I'd ever seen. My dad was so upset he wrote to *National Geographic* and cancelled our subscription.

I'm sure that's why I want to be cremated. I don't ever want to look like that.

She takes out another cigarette, but doesn't light it.

Let me explain something to you. I'm a working actor, and that's no small feat. The 'working' part. But take a good look at me and ask yourself, 'Is this a Juliet?' and the answer is ... no, of course not, I'm not *pretty* enough, you see? I am what is referred to as a character actor, which is the polite way of saying I'm technically proficient but I don't make teenage boys come in their pants. Fair. But I can be the best friend, I won't *threaten* anyone, yes? I can play the Shakespearean bawds. But my name will never go above the title.

She smiles.

Jonathan and I started dating when I was twenty-nine. And today, I might ask myself, 'How did you ever fall for this man?' But back then, my thirties were just up ahead, looming on the horizon, *louring* ... Two things happened: first, I realized that if I wanted more than half-hearted fuck friendships with other character actors, I needed to start looking for a relationship. And second – ladies? – my ovaries were aching in a vicious kind of way. I mean, by that point I was spending lots of time with my niece and nephew, and my sister kept telling me, 'Children are wonderful, children will change your life,' blah blah blah. So she introduces me to her husband's friend, Dr. Jonathan Fahey, a leading expert in glaciology – so says Google. And, okay, he's maybe not the guy I'd pick out in a lineup, but then again ...

Points at her own face.

And he's lovely, he's reliable, he's good with the twins, they love him, he wants a family, he's stable, everyone's like, 'He's such a great guy,' yadda yadda yadda ... So the sex isn't earth-shattering ...

Judith shrugs.

After all – and I'm quoting him here – 'hedonism is the purview of our twenties.'

I mean ... 'purview?'

There are days when I wonder what he saw in me. I think I was exotic. *Artsy.* Maybe the one thing we have in common is that we have no idea what the other one does for a living.

I marry him because I will finally have some stability in my life. We buy a house, fix it up, I start to 'nest.' I talk to my menstrual blood, I make promises: 'It won't be long now.'

And then, my sister and her husband are driving home one evening and they're about to go under an overpass when – for absolutely no good reason – a giant piece of the overpass cracks off and crushes them both.

Boom.

And it's tragic because – well, yes, because they're dead – but also because no one dies like that. That's how the Road

Runner dies, okay? It's a fucking cartoon death. People don't die like that, right? Wrong.

Judith lights the cigarette.

It's the coyote that dies. Not the Road Runner. The Road Runner always gets away ...
Meep meep.

Takes a long drag from her cigarette.

Of course we adopt Tanya and Thomas. Of course. Jonathan loves them, they love him, it's easy. Well, as easy as it can be under the circumstances. Overnight, we become parents to two preteens. We build a bunk bed in the baby room. And guess what? My ovaries are *pissed*. Maybe next year, says Jonathan. Maybe next year, I tell my period.
Yeah, well. We all know how that goes.
Then last year, Thomas drowns ...

Judith puts out her half-finished cigarette.

It's hard not to think, on some level, that this family is cursed. Because – come on! What the fuck is that? That's a sick fucking sense of humour.
But maybe, maybe now we can think about having one of our own. Tanya's fourteen, so ... so it's a possibility, it's an *option*. Right? Right. Only, now, 'climate change' is important, I mean, you film one PowerPoint presentation and people get real worked up about it. And I'm not an idiot, I *understand* the problem. I *get* it. But when you're married to one of the world's leading glaciology experts? Icebergs are a big deal, glaciers are a big deal, Greenland is a big fucking deal, but the state of your wife's reproductive organs ... ?

Well.

He calls me, from whatever middle-of-nowhere armpit town he's staying in, and he tells me about this island he's discovered. And there's something in his voice – excitement? I can't quite put my finger on it. And he says, 'Judith, come visit. Bring Tanya and come see this place ... '

Judith puts up her index finger.

'Sweetheart, it's so beautiful, it's this beautiful barren landscape ...'

I cry when he says that. Because that's me, he's just described *me* ... and that something in his voice? It's *love*, paternal love, the love one gives to something one has birthed, but that love belongs *to me*. Me. Me. No one else. Not that toothless skank whore Greenland, not *her*. It's not fair.

It's not. Fair.

Judith lights a new cigarette.

He didn't have the ... the decency? The delicacy? To consider, just ... consider ... naming it after me. Who the fuck am I, right?

Yeah.

Takes a long drag from her cigarette.

So I call David. He's one of my ex-fuck-friend character actors, and I invite myself over. I like him because we have this game, he calls me his 'little whore' and that's how he fucks me. And he never says 'please' and he never says 'thank you.'

Judith looks out, her expression impassive.

TANYA

Tanya reads a book on Greenland. She makes a note on an index card. She holds up a picture.

Fact: Greenland's coat of arms looks like a kung fu fighting polar bear.

Tanya karate chops.

Hi-yah!
Probably to remind people that this is a country that will kick your ass!

Tanya gauges the audience.

Yeah, that's how I'll start my presentation.
Jonathan says a joke or anecdote is a great way to grab people's attention.
I was gonna start with a different joke ... okay, okay – a tourist asks a little boy, 'Is it ever warm in Greenland?' and the little boy says, 'How should I know? I'm only thirteen.'
Yeah, right? *Totally* funny – but when I told it to Aunt Judy, she didn't get it. I'm talking crickets here. Not even a ha ha, aren't you adorable kinda thing. Nope. What I did get was, 'I know where you got *that* joke.'
She is, as my mom used to say, a wet blanket.

Looks at the coat of arms.

Well, maybe the kung fu'll make her smile. If Aunt Judy smiles, a normal human being will probably laugh.

Tanya karate chops.

Hi-yah!

This whole 'show and tell' business is for Miss Peach's class and yes, that's her real name, and no, I don't think it's cute. 'Do a presentation on the country of your choice, and include some interesting facts and/or mythology.' Okay, first of all, who says 'and/or'? Like, really? And second, she's all 'do your research and use the library' and it's like, lady, have you even heard of Wikipedia? And this thing called copy-paste? She is so old-school.

Tanya looks down at her book.

Fact: Melanie Green is *also* doing Greenland, but only because she thinks it has something to do with her name. Which obviously it doesn't.

If that's what she wants, she should do her report on Switzerland. It's a country with a lot of cows.

Anyway, everyone knows that Melanie Green always does her homework at the last minute. And that means she'll be copy-pasting, ergo, her presentation will lack rigour. Which is why *I'm* using a book.

I bet you a thousand dollars she comes in and pulls out the Erik the Red story, you know, how he named it Green-land to trick people into thinking he'd found farmable land?

Fact: I asked Jonathan and that story is *apocryphal*, meaning it's of doubtful origin. He said if it's true, then Erik the Red was a marketing genius. Which he probably wasn't, since he was a Viking.

You're probably wondering why Miss Peach let two people do Greenland since Melanie picked it first. Well. Miss Peach, as it happens, feels really really guilty because on the first day of school, she was doing roll call and apparently someone in administration put their stupid pants on, because she called out my name, Tanya Morrissey, and then she called out, Thomas Morrissey.

The class goes super quiet, and Miss Peach calls out his name again. Everyone is looking at me, like, am I going to say anything? Cry, what? Finally Christine gets up and whispers something to Miss Peach, who turns as red as a beet. She's all like, 'I'm sorry,' and goes on with roll call. Anyway, she's been very very *very* nice to me since then. Like, so nice I wanna say, 'Back off!' you know?

Oh, and the next day? In the cafeteria? I'm in line behind Nadia Byer, and she takes one of the last two Jell-Os, right? And she says, 'You can share the last one with Thomas.'

Tanya shakes her head.

Well, I just went ahead and punched her in the boob. Hard. She cried, and actually told on me. Okay, sure, I got detention for a week, but she got three days for what she said.

Anyway, now I kinda feel bad for her. Apparently when Ryan Duncan drew a penis in class she actually gagged, so some of the guys started calling her 'Nads,' and ... Well, she's not *petite*, right? So in Phys Ed, she's not the most graceful ... Sometimes she has trouble, you know, doing things and so now people whisper, 'Go, Nads, go! Go, Nads, go! Go, Nads, go!' and it's horrible, I mean, totally cruel.

Once I said it too, I didn't even realize, you know? I was just saying it.

Tanya shrugs and returns to her book.

Fact: Greenland is approximately 83.1 percent water, which is the most of any inhabited country. Most of that, obviously, is the glacier.

So now I'm reading about the different creation myths of Greenland and – can you believe it? Some of them involve twins ...

Tanya mouths 'Hello?'

Their names were Malina and Anningan. (Not to like harp on this, but Melanie Green does not have any siblings.) Anyway, according to this book, one night, the sister, Malina, carrying a torch, sneaks into her brother's tent and puts ash on his face while he's asleep. (And I believe it because it's something Thomas and I would totally do.) But then Anningan wakes up and discovers what his sister has done, so he gets up and chases after Malina, and they run sooo fast that they fly up into the sky, and to this day the ash-covered Anningan chases the torch-bearing Malina.

They're like the sun and the moon, you know? It's *poetic*.

Tanya picks up one of the index cards.

Fact: Greenland has the lowest population density in the world: 0.26 people per square kilometre. It's like having four kilometres between every person living there.

I've never actually been to Greenland, but I kinda have. I mean, in my imagination I have. You know the show, *The Amazing Race*? Well, Thomas and I came up with our own version. It's so cool.

Tanya gets a large map of the world.

Okay, so the idea is that we pick a country that we're going to 'visit' that day. So, for example, he'd pick India. It's hot there, so we'd put on our bathing suits and run around the house, and when Aunt Judy asked us what we were doing we'd be like, 'We're in India!' And we'd draw the Taj Mahal and that would be our pictures, and we'd bug Jonathan to take us to an Indian restaurant ...

And we went to Greenland once, I remember, because it was the middle of summer but we put on our winter coats and went to the park and rolled around in the grass. *Totally* wrong. We should've stuck our heads in the freezer.

Fact: There are no Greenlandic restaurants in Toronto.

Fact: Greenlanders eat walrus heart. It's a delicacy.

Fact: Eating walrus heart is *gross*.

Okay.

I'm going to tell you something, but you won't believe me. And I know it's hard to believe, I know that because if it didn't happen to me I'm not sure I'd believe it but it's absolutely true. I knew Thomas was dead because my heart *broke*. It – it actually cracked, it made a cracking sound, I heard it, and Aunt Judy said she heard it too.

You don't believe me, do you? Well, that's your loss. It's *poetic*.

Tanya flips to a new index card.

Fact: The official language of Greenland is Greenlandic, which is also known as Kalaallisut.

Ka. Laa. Li. Sut. That is a great word for the breath game. Thomas and I played it all the time. You have to say the word as many times as possible on a single breath.

Tanya takes a deep breath and counts with her fingers as she says 'Kalaallisut' as many times as she can.

Phew! Thomas is really, really good at this game. Was.

You know, I don't understand why people are weird about saying his name around me. Like maybe it would hurt me? But that doesn't make any sense, because when someone says 'Thomas,' I think, 'Oh yeah, he's my twin brother.' And I have all these great memories of us together.

Like travelling the world. That was fun.

When Aunt Judy told us we were going to Florida for vacation, Thomas and I were both totally *not* excited. I mean, Florida? Can you think of anywhere more boring? *Everyone's* been to Florida.

We were both like, take us somewhere more exciting, please! Like, I don't know, the Maldives! Do you know anyone who's been there? Exactly. I mean, Aunt Judy didn't even know where it was. *That's* the kinda place we wanted to go to.

Tanya shrugs.

Nope. Florida.

And you know what? Florida sucks. At least we won't be going back there anytime soon. I mean ...

Yeah.

Tanya picks up a new index card.

Fact: The weight of Greenland's ice sheet ...

Tanya puts down the index card.

Sometimes people do really, really, *really* stupid things. Like name an island Thomas Morrissey Island. Because you don't know Thomas, you don't know what he was like. So when someone says his name, then your association, your connection is going to be, 'Thomas Morrissey, oh yeah, isn't that the island that appeared off the coast of Greenland because of GLOBAL WARMING? That's like a horrible catastrophe!'

Do you see what I'm saying? It's like naming your child Chernobyl. Or Hiroshima. Not a good idea.

Anyway, it's all okay because Jonathan got a phone call from the Greenland government today. They decided that he couldn't name the island in English, but had to find a name in Kalaallisut. So he called it ...

Tanya picks up a piece of paper.

Uunartoq Qeqertaq. It has a nice ring to it, no? It means 'The Warming Island,' which is way better.

Tanya counts the syllables on her fingers.

Six syllables. That's a tough one.

Tanya takes a deep breath and counts with her fingers as she says 'Uunartoq Qeqertaq.' After the second repetition, she notices the map of Greenland. On the same breath:

Jonathan showed me where it is ...

Tanya looks at the map of Greenland as she repeats, 'Uunartoq Qeqertaq.' Points to the island and exhales.

There, right there. It looks like a little claw, or three little fingers ...

She takes a pen and circles the island, then writes the name beside it.

You know what? This is probably the world's most up-to-date map of Greenland.

The coolness of it hits her.

Maybe it's the *only* up-to-date map of Greenland there is!

Tanya looks at the map.

Whoa. This is *unique*. And you might think having something unique is easy, but it's hard. I often have thoughts, you know, that I think are 100 percent original? But then I'll tell Christine and she's like, 'I was totally thinking that!'

But this ...

Oh. My. God. Sometimes, I have moments of genius. I mean, real genius.

Melanie Green can keep Greenland. Because I'm going to do my presentation on ...

Tanya holds the map up to the audience.

Fact: Uunartoq Qeqertaq was discovered by my uncle, Jonathan Fahey, off the coast of Greenland.

Fact: No one lives on the island. Yet.

Fact: If you did, you would see narwhals from your kitchen window.

Fact ...

Fact: Uunartoq Qeqertaq needs a creation myth.

Okay ... so ... There once were two twins, Aynat and Samoht, who lived on Greenland. They shared the island with a grizzly bear, Nahtanoj, who was also their guardian – because Aynat and Samoht had a tendency to get into trouble. One time, they decided to surprise him. They hid behind a rock and when Nahtanoj passed by, Aynat and Samoht jumped in front of him and yelled, 'Surprise!' He was so scared that his fur turned totally white and then he became so angry that he sent Aynat and Samoht to their rooms. But he couldn't do that, because Greenland was a flat island and there were no walls. So Nahtanoj brought them to the edge of the island and used his big claw to slash off a piece of land, which became Uunartoq Qeqertaq. He then cut off his baby toe and dropped it in the ocean, where it became a narwhal. And the narwhal carried Aynat and Samoht to Uunartoq Qeqertaq, where they were grounded for three days and three nights.

Aynat and Samoht played different games to pass the time, but soon they were bored. And that's when Samoht said, 'Let's go for a swim.' Aynat was scared, because it was the one thing they were forbidden. But Samoht didn't listen, as usual. He took a deep breath and dove into the ocean. Aynat waited and waited and waited for Samoht to come back, and when it was clear that he wasn't going to, a great big sound shook the earth ... It was

Aynat's heart, breaking in two ... Aynat began to cry, and her tears fell into the ocean, where they froze and became icebergs that floated away ... and she's still there now, Aynat, she's still ...

Lights up on Judith, smoking, and Jonathan, nursing his drink.

She's still ...

Tanya brings herself back to a calm place.

Fact: I thought this would be *poetic*. But it's not.

Do you ever wonder if there's a word, a kind of password or a name or something, that if you kept saying it over and over you'd never run out of breath? Like, maybe the thing you loved most in the world. If you just keep saying it over and over, you could keep breathing, no matter what?

I know, it's stupid, but I just wonder, I guess.

Tanya takes a deep breath and counts with her fingers, slowly, as she mouths a secret word.

Judith and Jonathan are lost in their own thoughts, their own worlds.

BLACKOUT.

ICELAND

ICELAND

Iceland premiered at the SummerWorks Theatre Festival on August 10, 2012, with the following artistic team:

Kassandra: Christine Horne
Halim: Kawa Ada
Anna: Claire Calnan

Director: Ravi Jain
Production Designer: Joanna Yu
Lighting Designer: Kim Purtell
Sound Designer: Richard Feren
Stage Managers: Kat Chin and Neha Ross
Assistant Director: Jenna Turk
Producer: Renna Reddie

Winner of the 2012 SummerWorks Prize for Best New Play

Iceland subsequently opened at the Factory Theatre on March 7, 2013, with the following artistic team:

Kassandra: Lauren Vandenbrook
Halim: Kawa Ada
Anna: Claire Calnan

Director: Ravi Jain
Production Designer: Joanna Yu
Lighting Designer: Kim Purtell
Sound Designer: Richard Feren
Stage Manager: Neha Ross
Assistant Director: Jenna Turk

NOTE ON ICELAND

Each monologue is interrupted, at various moments, by dialogue spoken by a different actor.

These interruptions are not meant to be played as naturalistic conversations; rather, they are the memory of the character whose monologue is being spoken, and his or her response is indicated with quotation marks.

KASSANDRA: And then, there's no more shouting, it's quiet. I hide in the bathtub, but it's not good hiding place because the shower drape is clear plastic, you can see right through ...

The door opens and I think it's the john coming to get me. But no. It's a woman. His wife? She walk right past me, like she doesn't see me. It's hard to not notice someone sitting inside the bathtub. But she doesn't.

Instead, she pulls up her skirt and pulls down underwear, and sits on the toilet and urinates. Then she does something very strange. She turns left and makes to grab some toilet paper. But toilet paper is on the right. When she realize this, she stop and put her head in her hands, and she cries.

I think this is good time to leave, and that's when she look up and sees me.

She doesn't say anything. Just stares at me.

I notice this woman doesn't wear a ring. The john doesn't either, so maybe she is just girlfriend. She is shaking a little bit.

I get up. And that's when she speaks –

ANNA: Who are you?

KASSANDRA: Her voice is calm. This make me very nervous. No, it make me very scared. And it's silly, but ever since I was little girl, I can't lie when I'm scared. My parents say, 'We have lied all our life so that you don't have to.'

ANNA: Who are you?

KASSANDRA: I say, 'I am Kassandra.'

It's my real name. Mattias say it's dangerous to tell anyone our real name, but as I said: I can't lie when I'm scared.

The woman look at me, look at the way I am dressed. She frown when she sees that I am wearing only lingerie. I feel like little animal caught in a flashlight. I can't move a muscle.

ANNA: Did he hurt you?

KASSANDRA: This is not what I expect her to say.

It make me feel a bit better. I begin to doubt that she is his girlfriend. This is not a question that a girlfriend would ask.

I shake my head. She says –

ANNA: Is he your boyfriend?

KASSANDRA: I say, 'No.'

She nod like somehow this explain everything.

She remember then that she is on the toilet. She looks at me and has ... Punastab?

She touches her cheek.

Turn very red? I can't remember the word.

I say, 'Okay, I'll leave you.'

She doesn't look at me or say anything, so I step out of the bathtub and leave.

I close the door behind me, and I remember then that my dress is still inside the bathroom. I must wait for the woman to finish before I leave.

I turn around. I see the john lying on the floor, and the carpet is stain with blood. At first, I think he's dead, but then I notice there are little bubbles of blood on his lips – he is still breathing, but with much difficulty.

I understand now why the woman was shaking ... Maybe the john attack her and she defend herself? Or maybe she ... ?

I must call for help. I look for my purse. It's stuck under the ... lower leg? The calf, yes? The calf of the john. My phone is in my purse.

It takes a few pulls to get it loose.

I take out my phone and press nine and one and then I remember Mattias tell me that I must never call police from my phone, that it could be trace back to me. If I need to call ambulance, I must use the john's phone.

But I do not see his cellphone.

That is when I realize that I am in big trouble.

My fingerprint are everywhere in the apartment. If I call for help, they will have a record of my voice.

And they come find me, they will arrest me and I am just on student visa, so of course they will deport me – even if I explain what happen, they will not believe me because ...

She stops.

My mother, she is history professor. This is why she name me Kassandra, the Greek woman who is cursed by gods with power to tell the future but no one ever believe her. 'Exactly like history professor,' Memm say. I tell her, 'But I can't tell the future,' and she says, 'It's not so hard: just look at the past.' She's very proud when I tell her I want to become history professor like her. Perhaps it make up for Jannu, who –

She shakes her head.

Jannu is my twin brother. He nickname me 'Neetud,' which means 'cursed,' and I call him 'Pieru,' which is Estonian word for 'fart.' So we're fair.

She thinks.

We love each other very much, but I know Jannu is not the brightest boy in world.

When I go back to Estonia last summer, I just finish my first year of master's at U of T. And one night when I'm back, Jannu comes home and he is beat up, yes? He lose three teeth and one of his bone here –

She touches her orbital bone.

The eye bone? Orbit bone. It's broken. He won't tell us what happen. We take him to the hospital, and they call the police. But Jannu, he refuse to say anything about it.

I notice Memm is crying.

She takes this in.

I have never seen my mother cry, not even after Father pass away. I take her aside and ask her what is going on. She tells me that Jannu gambles. He spends his nights watching lots of television and now he thinks he can become world poker champion.

I do not say this out loud, but to myself I think, 'But he's such a bad liar!'

That is not worst part, Memm says. Jannu has borrowed money from the Obtshak, the Estonian mafia. And they have come to Memm's house about repaying Jannu's debt.

Memm say to me, 'It's not your problem.' That I must continue my study and make a life in Canada. But how can I do that? She is my mother. Jannu is my twin brother. My baby brother, because I am seven minutes older.

We were born on the Balti kett, it is in English the Baltic chain? August 23, 1989. Two million people gather to join, hand in hand, from Tallinn to Vilnius. A human chain 600 kilometres long. For peaceful support of independence of Estonia and Latvia and Lithuania. How do they organize this without Internet? I don't know.

And Memm was very pregnant back then; my father did not want her to go. But she yell at him, 'I am history professor! How do I not go?' That's my mother: she is very, um, 'donkey' when she want to be, yes? So they go to be part of the chain. How proud they were to be there! And then her water break. People around her panic, yes? They want her to go to the hospital. But my mother, she be like donkey again and say, 'I will not break the chain! My children will be born right here!' My father try to reason with her, but she refuse to let go of anyone's hand. A doctor is called, and a few hours after, me and my brother are born. We make the cover of *Eesti Ekspress:* 'The First Children of the Revolution!'

My mother swears she never let go of anyone's hand on the chain during the whole thing.

She shrugs.

However, she also say that me and Jannu come out holding hands. This we know is metaphor.

And this is why – why it's hard for me to let gambling debt not be my problem.

When Memm and Jannu bring me to the airport, I remember giving hug to Jannu and he say to me, 'You are so lucky, Kassa.' And I say, 'Why?' And he says, 'Because you live in a place that believes in meritocracy.' I laugh because Jannu not use big word like that very often. Memm laughs too, very loud. Jannu turn to her and says, 'What?' And she says, 'There is no meritocracy in a country that sell lottery tickets.' As I hug her goodbye, I promise to send money to help them.

She takes a deep breath.

Back in Toronto, I go to Student Services and ask about jobs available. There are a few jobs on campus, and a couple of coffee shops have positions. But when I ask how much I make ... I'm sorry, but it does not add up. The math. Maybe if I work full-time ... But how can I study if I'm busy forty hours? No. I must find work that pays better for not as many hours.

She looks away, embarrassed.

There are not many jobs like that. One of my roommates tells me that stripping maybe is good. Some places treat girls okay. But they say, no, you don't have big enough breasts. Maybe if you get a boob job.

She shakes her head.

I work at massage parlour for little bit. Money is okay, but I work very late hours. It affect my study.

And then one day, I work on client, Mattias. Unlike most people, he does not assume that I'm Russian. He begins to talk to me in Estonian. We realize we are both from the same area, and that his cousin is friend of mine.

This is a very strange conversation, because I'm holding his penis the whole time.

Mattias own an escort agency and I begin to work there. Because we are both Estonian, he protect me and I can choose my own schedule. I work ten hours a week and make enough to live and send my mother money every month. I tell her it's a bursary I win for history paper.

Of course I am ashamed that I lie to my mother. But what else can I do?

Her hands clench into fists.

I came here to teach history. I came here to become a Canadian and marry a good man and raise a family. I work hard. I am good person. So how did I go from that to standing in a stranger's apartment, in my underwear, with a dying man on the floor ... ? Jumal aita mind! If police find me here I will be deported, or worse if they think I do it ... ? But I must help him, yes? I must. There are little bubbles on his lips, he is still breathing ... What must I do?

She puts her head in her hands.

HALIM: Okay, you want some advice? Here it is, free of charge: never buy anything Russian except for vodka and hookers. Maybe it's some kind of communist mojo in the water, but the vodka's potent and the women can suck dick like *nobody's* business.

Let me tell you about ... uh ... forgot her name. Anyway, she is a *hot* little number, this one.

It's a tricky price point, the three-hundred-dollar hooker. You know they'll be groomed and have all their teeth, but that doesn't necessarily mean they're gonna be head-turners. But occasionally ... it works out. More bang for your buck, am I right?

He laughs.

Yeah, nothing? Okay.

Anyway, I ask her, 'You're Russian, right?' And she says –

KASSANDRA: Yes. You are businessman?

HALIM: I don't want to overcomplicate things, but let's be clear about something: 'businessman' is a useless fucking word. Because who isn't one today? A drug dealer? Businessman. A pimp? Businessman. *Plumber?* You get the idea.

I'm in real estate. But that – that doesn't – okay. I know we don't like to use the c-word in this country, but let's call a spade a spade: I'm a Capitalist, okay? The capital-C, free-market type. Why? Because capitalism rocks. And if you think otherwise, well, hey, I'm sure you're a nice person but you're a complete fucking idiot. Sorry.

So, as I was saying, why overcomplicate things?

'Yeah, sure,' I said, 'I'm a "businessman."'

KASSANDRA: What kind of business?

HALIM: 'I flip houses, and no, I'm not gonna explain what that is.'

Because right now, let's be honest, time is money. And that's when she says –

KASSANDRA: What can I do for you?

HALIM: See? Now that, that is a thing of beauty. If you've ever asked yourself, 'Why is money good?' then here's your answer: it simplifies everything.

This 'relationship' is simple: She is the hooker. I am the john.

Service provider. Customer.

Supply. Demand.

Seller. Buyer.

That's it.

Straightforward. Uncomplicated. Symbiotic.

You know what money is? Money is perfect.

Oh, and then – this is a good one – I ask her, 'You take cheques, right?'

KASSANDRA: Uh ... no.

HALIM: 'Oh for fuck's – It's a joke!'

He takes out a money clip.

Christ! Russians.

Wallets, for the record, are fucking useless. Why bother? No one can see you've got money, while this –

He waves the money clip.

Each and every one of you is looking at my money right now, am I right? Of course you are. There's no shame. This means business. Would you fuck with a guy who carries a money clip? Exactly.

So, back to the question. What can she do for me?

Well, let's see ... You wanna give her the right idea, you know? Some guidance, something she can relate to. For example: 'I want you to suck my dick like ... like we're on the bread line and I'm holding the very last loaf.'

He grins.

Epic!

I can tell that some of your delicate sensibilities have been ruffled. And I know this is Canada and everything, but I'm not gonna apologize.

He raises his palm in a conciliatory gesture.

Look, let's keep some perspective. She has a skill that I do not possess. Therefore, I am paying for said skill. Very well, I might add. And I'm a good tipper.

You all good tippers out there?

My point isn't about tipping. My point is that every left-wing, bleeding-heart, Jack-Layton-bobblehead-owning liberal has a dirty little secret that they keep tucked away, out of view, in the hopes that no one will ever find out that deep down, they're a Capitalist at heart. That's right. Every. One of 'em.

Of course, they'll deny it. It's like that story about, was it Churchill? I think so. He asks this lady, 'Will you sleep with me for a million pounds?' And she thinks for a moment and says, 'Yes.' Then Churchill says, 'Will you sleep with me for five pounds?' and she's like, 'Mr. Churchill, what kind of woman do you think I am?' and he says, 'We've already established that, now we're just negotiating.'

He laughs.

I love that story! And my point is, if somebody offered me a million bucks to fuck them? Uh, yeah. Sure, my price point is higher than the hooker's, but we're not different.

And liberals fucking hate to hear that. But the truth is, they're just as scared about the stock market tanking, because they're invested. Ethical funds, sure. Or in real estate. But in any case, they're looking for the same thing: a profit. Buy low, sell high. And that's capital-C Capitalism, ladies and gents.

Sure, ten years ago you could get away with a savings account, when interest rates paid 5.25 percent. But today? Please.

He laughs.

I went on a date once with this smoking hot chick. We rented *Indecent Proposal*, you know, where Robert Redford offers what's-her-name, G.I. Jane, a million bucks to sleep with him. And she does. Afterwards, we're both like 'Yeah, it was pretty good, I liked it,' et cetera, but then I realize she likes it because, quote, 'In the end, it was about love and fidelity.' I'm thinking, 'You're fucking crazy,' but I keep my cool and say that no, really it's about money and capitalism. She's like, 'What? No. It's about how love can't be bought.' To which I respond, not unreasonably, 'She fucked him for a million dollars, and then left her husband to be with him!' And she says, 'But she goes back to her husband because she loves him!' And I say – okay, I may have raised my voice a little bit – 'She goes back to her husband because women are fucking irrational!'

That didn't go over so well.

He shakes his head.

Too bad. She was so *hot*.

Anyway, this is a good example of, of the thing that annoys me, that drives me fucking crazy, *actually*, with 'progressives' in general. It's not that they disagree with me – hell, I disagree with lots of people – but that they don't have the balls to stare reality in the face. I mean, they're incapable of taking a good hard look at the truth of the world that they're living in.

Okay, for example: my latest flip.

He gestures to show the apartment.

Nice one-bedroom in Liberty Village. You know why it's called that, by the way? Liberty Village? It's in honour of the countless yuppies saddled with twenty-five-year mortgages. Who says condo developers don't have a sense of humour? Anyway, I bought the unit for a song from some overleveraged dumb-ass from Buffalo. He had buyers lined up, but he sold it to me. Why? Because I could pay cash: less waiting, less paperwork, less headaches.

Eh? Un-complicated.

From there, it's just a question of making a few cosmetic changes, staging it properly, and then – ta-da! 'Spectacular premium one-bedroom in the heart of trendy Liberty Village, floor-to-ceiling windows and cozy balcony with a view of the lake. Chef-inspired kitchen with granite countertops and stainless-steel appliances. Bathroom upgraded with rainforest shower. Perfect for the urban professional!'

Yeah. 'Rainforest shower.'

He shrugs; he has no idea what that means.

It's not going to win a prize, okay, but it will net me a forty to sixty k profit in about a month, thank you very much.

He smiles.

Anyway, so the flip – this stupid woman, she comes to visit the condo ...

He thinks.

Actually, that's probably not fair, because I think she might be mildly retarded or something. Asperger's or whatever. Wouldn't look me in the eye.

Anyway, she comes in and goes over the place like she's some kind of forensic house inspector or whatever.

Thirty. Five. Minutes. Seriously, thirty-five minutes in a one-bedroom apartment. I'm exhausted just thinking about it.

And then you know what she says? She can't 'afford' it. What. The. Fuck. *Is* that?

Seriously. Now, let me be clear: I'm not pissed off because she wasted my time. Well, okay, a little bit. But that's not the main thing. The main thing is – of course she can afford it! But she *chooses* not to. In her mind, she's thinking, 'Oh, I'm poor, but I'm gonna visit an apartment I can't afford anyway 'cause a girl can always dream ... ' And that may sound reasonable until you realize that this is the same girl who drinks fair-trade, organic, shade-grown, hand-picked, wind-power-roasted coffee. If any of you got a warm fuzzy feeling about that, you should know that you're paying three times what a normal human being pays for coffee.

He processes this thought.

It's fucking *coffee*.

And then she comes crying when she doesn't have money to buy a house? Please. She *chooses* not to be able to afford it. If she took a good hard look at the truth of the world that she's living in, maybe she'd realize that we're living in an age of easy credit. That, by the way, is not a dirty word when it allows you to buy a fucking house.

But no, she'd rather buy five-dollar coffee and feel good about herself. Well, you know what? That's fucking stupid. She can get on her bike and pedal back to Parkdale. While she can still afford to live there.

I know some of you are thinking, 'Now hold on there, bucko! Did you not see what happened down in the States?' Well, yeah, kinda did. But you're blaming the wrong people. Credit is not inherently good or bad – it's just credit. People, on the other hand, can be smart, stupid or absolutely fucking moronic. And it's that last group that I wish would learn the cardinal fucking rule: DO. THE. MATH. If you don't, then I'm sorry, but shut the fuck up because that's exactly like walking into a bank, buck naked, holding a sign that says, 'Fuck me up the ass for 5 percent down!' and then later turning around and saying, 'Uh, hold on a minute, I think I was raped.'

He looks at the audience: 'Come on!'

Yeah yeah yeah, I know, you're thinking: 'Easy for you to say, Gandhi, you're good at math.'

Hey, that's racist. I'm Pakistani.

He laughs.

It was a *joke*! I mean, I *am* Pakistani – like, I was born here, but, just, Gandhi was Indian ...

Shakes his head.

Oh, and that retarded woman? Totally uncomfortable that I'm, you know, 'ethnic.' All the little tell-tale signs. If you don't know what I'm talking about, it's because you're white.

Though on some level – and, please, I'm used to it – but on some level she's better, well, no, she's more honest than those white people (because it's always white people) who act all friendly and polite 'cause they wouldn't, you know, want you to think that they're racist or anything.

Oh yes you are. And oh, we know.

To be clear, the moral of this story ain't, 'Do the math and don't be a racist.' Although that's good advice. But no. The moral here is that there's only one thing in this world that is perfect.

He takes out his money clip.

Perfect, because it's a perfect reflection of its owner. If you're an idiot, that's what your money will be. If you're a smart guy?

Waves the money.

Exactly.

He thinks, then nods.

My guess is that you've never heard of Dick Burnett. He's an expert on real estate tax liens, and while that may not *sound* exciting ...

He grins.

I went to his conference in Vegas a few years ago, just around the time the mortgage collapse was starting. I had a, an intuition that it was gonna be big. So I signed up at the last minute, and I paid an arm and a leg for my hotel 'cause it was the same weekend as the big porn convention.

So I'm there with like about fifty other guys in one of the smaller conference rooms at the Candlewood, and this big fat bastard goes up on stage, takes the mic, and says, 'I guess all the women are at the *other* convention.'

He laughs.

And then he says, 'What've you all asked Santa for for Christmas?' A few of us giggle, you know, like, what the fuck? But he repeats the question, and some guy shouts out, 'Pussy!'

Dick Burnett shakes his head, like we're a class of mildly retarded children.

'This,' he says, 'is what you should all be asking Santa for.'

And on the screen behind him appears a map of Iceland.

'Santa's feeling mighty generous this year, boys, courtesy of over-leveraged Icelandic fishmongers. I wanna be clear: bless 'em for trying; we all get a kick at the can. And they came out swinging: they privatized and deregulated their banks. There wasn't a debt obligation they didn't like and buy on the spot. It was Christmas 24/7 in Reykjavik! But there is always a reckoning; the Lord giveth and the Lord taketh away, gentlemen. And Icelanders must've slept through history class, because this is exactly how their fishing industry collapsed. You're going to make a boatload of money because you can put lipstick on a pig, boys, and you can dress a fisherman in a suit. But the pig's still a pig, and the fisherman ... '

And then Dick Burnett puts his hands together, like this, and says, 'Let's praise God for Iceland, where they don't know the difference between 'fish net' and 'net worth,' where they fail to understand that 'overleveraging' isn't about getting older, and where there live the greediest and dumbest motherfuckers to ever handle a derivative. Lord, grant us wealth so that by this time next year, we'll all be able to afford a suite at the Sands Hotel and have the porn stars knocking on *our* door. Amen.'

Give the man credit for showmanship.

That night, I run into Dick Burnett at the bar and I offer to buy him a drink.

Halim raises his hand in mock-toast.

'To Iceland.'

'Hear, hear,' Dick says and downs his drink. 'Hey, can I ask you a personal question?'

'Sure.'

'Halim. You're a Muslim?'

I nod and say, 'Not a very good one.'

'I gathered as much from the Scotch in your hand. Lapsed Baptist myself. More of a Benny Frankist these days.'

'A what?'

Dick Burnett chuckles, pulls out a hundred-dollar bill from his money clip –

He smiles.

– and lays it flat on the bar.

'The Benny Frankist believes in the higher power of the c-note, my friend. Is there anything in the world as powerful and versatile as this piece of paper? It is omnipotence incarnate. You want to eat at the finest establishments? You want to drive the fastest cars? Fuck the prettiest girls? Ask, and it shall be given you; seek, and ye shall find; knock, and it shall be opened unto you.'

He puts his hand on my shoulder.

'And if that's not enough, you can expunge your guilt by donating it to charity. You'll even get a tax receipt for your troubles. See? He's a good and loving God. He even has a Muslim and a Baptist drinking together in Vegas!'

I notice at this point that Dick's looking over at a tall redhead sitting at a table. She smiles at him.

I lean in and whisper, 'Hooker?'

'Son, I'm a 350-pound fat fuck named Dick. Yeah, she's a hooker.'

And I gotta say, I have a lot of respect for Dick in that moment, because here's a man who stares reality right in the eyes.

Then Dick says, 'I hope she swallows.'

I take a look at the redhead again.

'Not a chance.'

'Ye of little faith, Halim. Trust in the Benny Frank. If she's not amenable, then pull one of these puppies out and show it to her so she knows you mean business. And tell her that if she swallows, this'll be her tip.'

I ask him, 'It works?'

He looks over at the redhead again. 'Luke 12:43: "Blessed is that servant whom his master will find so doing when he comes."'

Dick folds his hundred-dollar bill into a small square: 'I always ask them to stick out their tongues when I'm done. And when they do ... '

He makes a gesture reminiscent of the Eucharist, using the folded bill as host.

'I call it giving Holy Communion.'

I say, 'That's a perfect metaphor for the banking crisis.'

Dick chuckles, then shakes his head. 'That's not quite right, actually. Because in the banking crisis, it's the whore who's gonna be paying us for the privilege!'

Halim laughs.

He's pretty quick on his feet!

It makes sense, though, doesn't it? I mean, you hear

liberals go on and on about equality, they go on and on about unions and affirmative action and all that communist bullshit. Change the world! Sure. End poverty! Yup. People first! Okay.

But when someone walks in, slaps his money clip down on the table and says, 'Who's ready to swallow?' Well, you don't have to ask twice.

Here's the cold, hard truth of the world that we're living in: abstract ideas, ethics, morals don't stand a chance against a pile of cold, hard cash.

Hey, look: I put my money where her mouth is.

He laughs, hard.

Oh, that reminds me of – Okay, so the Russian hooker, you know, she's giving me head and I ask her, 'Hey. What's your name again?' and just as she's about to answer, I say, 'Don't talk with your mouth full!'

He laughs.

Aw, come on! News flash: it's not the nicest or prettiest or smartest person who wins.

He waves his money clip.

Okay, okay. Here's a better one. What is communism doing *right now*?

He grins.

It's sucking my dick!

He laughs.

Oh for fuck's sake. Is there some kind of veto on a sense of humour?

He scowls, annoyed.

Seriously, will you fucking laugh already?

ANNA: I have a question.

But before I say anything else, I want you to know that I am not special, or exceptional, or whatever. It feels strange having to say that, to pre-empt a conversation that way.

I'm sure you've noticed that the individual, or perhaps I should say, the – the ambition of individuality has become very fashionable lately. And the idea that we are all unique in our own way – which is true on a simplistic level – is not, I think, is not true in the greater sense. We are instruments, and there's no shame in that, right?

She thinks.

I had a guinea pig when I was a child. I called him Alphonse. Which is a great name, but my father always called him Al which drove me crazy and he'd say, 'Anna, don't be a banana.' It was his idea of a joke. Ha-ha-no.

Anyway, Alphonse was pretty smart for a guinea pig. I kept treats for him in one of my drawers, and whenever I opened it he'd squeak, you know, like guinea pigs do.

She imitates a guinea pig squeal.

Because he thought maybe I was gonna feed him, which I did sometimes but not always, you know, sometimes I was just getting a pair of … whatever, socks.

Point is, I let Alphonse out of his cage from time to time so he could run around my room, you know, stretch his stubby little legs and all that. But I kept the door shut because we lived on a farm and there's no way he'd survive out on his own – I mean, foxes and whatnot. He wasn't that smart.

But one time my mom opened the door while he was out and Alphonse made a run for it. Little bugger was quick, too.

We chased after him but he ran under the living room couch and we couldn't find him after that.

I cried. My mother comforted me, but I could tell she was getting impatient. Finally she said, 'Anna, enough. It's just a guinea pig,' which surprised me because she preached that God loved all living things. 'Some more than others, dear.'

I found Alphonse the next morning on the porch. He'd eaten something – fertilizer, I think – and he was not doing so good. I was racked with guilt. I never should have let him escape.

I made a nest in a shoebox and stored him under my bed. At first, he just pooped and barfed, and wouldn't eat anything. Then he was quiet and lay still.

The next morning my mom comes into my room and there is a, a sharp smell. And she doesn't say anything, she just kinda scowls, crinkles her nose and ...

She inhales in short, sharp sniffs.

I want to die I'm so embarrassed because of course I know what it is, so I just say, 'I tooted,' and my mom goes, 'Well, it doesn't smell like vanilla, dear.'

My mother is a blunt instrument.

By the third day my father comes to investigate and he finds Alphonse, pretty much on the doorstep of death: wheezing, you know, and his eyes fluttering open and shut. My father takes him away and my mother turns to me: 'How could you let that poor creature suffer?'

I tell her I thought I could nurse him back to health. She shakes her head and says, 'Do you think you get to decide about life and death, young lady? Shame on you, Anna Godwin. Shame on you. We. Are. Instruments.'

Anna clears her throat.

Anyway, that's not, I mean, I'm not here to talk about my guinea pig.

I was at the Sputnik Café, the little hipster place on King? Right. And I'm browsing the internet, but there's this guy at the next table, he's chatting up this girl, this lady friend of his, but I feel like every third word out of his mouth is either four letters long or a blaspheme. And I can't concentrate anymore.

I interrupt the guy and I say, 'Excuse me, but would you mind not taking the Lord's name in vain?' He turns to me and gives me a look, a kind of vapid, empty look – not unlike a cow, actually. And he says, 'Excuse me?' and I repeat myself. He shakes his head a little, like he's having a brain toot, and I think, 'No, not a cow, a donkey. He looks like a donkey.'

Anyway, he gives me the usual blah-blah-blah about free speech, mind my own business, et cetera, et cetera, and it's wonderful because all I do is keep my cool and say, 'I don't mean to upset you, I'm just asking,' and the lady friend puts her hand on his arm and tells him to let it go. The young man looks at her, and that's when it happens: the quick flush of the cheeks and the sharp rise of red in his face. Shame.

In that moment I love him because that's God showing him the error of his ways. Showing him that he's not special.

He goes back to talking to his lady friend but it's not the same, he's not so ... reckless anymore. He knows someone's listening, he knows someone's watching. This gives me hope: people can be changed by Christ's love, right?

Anyway, I'm at the café to use the internet; I'm in the market for a home. My dad's gonna try to help me out a bit with the down payment. He thinks it's best if I buy something. That's smart, you know, because it's an investment. And I can't sleep on my cousin's couch forever. So I'm going through MLS and I'm checking out different one-bedrooms in the area, and then – wham! There it is, staring me in the face.

At first I'm like ... Look, I was just living there, you know, like last month? But there's no doubt. It's my apartment up for sale. It looks different – it's been repainted, and a lot of fixtures and things have been changed. But there's a picture of the balcony, and there's my little hibachi that I'd forgotten to take with me. I check the address: suite 633.

Understand: this was my first apartment alone. I was ... happy. For two years, it was home. Until three months ago when, out of the blue, the owner calls me and says he has to sell the apartment – he was American, something about the market collapsing, blah-blah-blah. I don't understand much about that. Now the thing is, I'd expect the buyer to honour my lease, right? Except the guy who buys it decides that he wants to move in, so I'm stuck having to move out. Of my home.

And here we are, a month later, and now it's *for sale*.

I tweet about this, and everyone is appalled. My friend Rachel from Colorado messages me saying, 'Well, you're gonna visit, right?' And I message back, 'I can't afford it' and she says, 'Aren't you curious?' And yeah, of course I'm curious.

I call up the real estate agent because I am, it's true, I didn't lie, I am genuinely interested in buying it. The home that I love. He calls it a condo. We arrange a visit that very afternoon.

We meet at the coffee shop across from my place. The real estate agent is an Indian guy, but it's okay because he's dressed in a suit. He says –

HALIM: Can I get you anything?

ANNA: 'No thank you.'

I don't want him to get the wrong idea – this is a meeting, not a date.

Anyway, we go over to the apartment and in the elevator. I almost give myself away by pressing the button for the sixth floor. But I catch myself just in time, and the Indian guy presses it. Suddenly, I get worried because – what if I run into one of my neighbours? I never really spoke to any of them, but enough to nod. And I'm thinking, 'If they see me now, it's been long enough that one of them might be like, "Hey, it's been so long, where've you been?"'

She makes a small explosion with her hand.

There goes my cover.

But I don't run into anyone. So he lets me into the apartment. And ... Well, okay, it's a lot nicer. A lot. Nicer. Than when I lived there. I mean, we're talking an upgrade from IKEA to Martha Stewart.

And the guy, the Indian guy, he notices that I'm looking pretty closely at all the little details that have changed, you know, cupboard handles and the like ...

I say, 'The owner's done a really great job with the place.' And he says –

HALIM: Thank you.

ANNA: 'Thank you.'

It takes my brain a second to process that. 'Thank you.' He's the owner. This guy, this Indian guy who is a real estate agent, is the guy who bought my home. Who was going to 'live' here, and is now selling it.

'You're the owner?'

HALIM: Yes. And you know, what I love is that I sell homes, not condos, but homes, places where people really feel like it's the place for them. I think that's very important, and –

ANNA: Blah-blah-blah, but all I'm thinking is, 'You dirty piece of shit –'

She inhales sharply.

Oh no. I'm so sorry. I can't believe I said that.

Anna rummages through her purse.
She takes out a half-eaten bar of soap.
She bites off a piece and chews it.

Honestly.

She puts the soap back in her purse.

Sorry.
    This man took my home from me.
    Anyway, he's going on but I stop listening to him and think very, very bad things. But I remain calm, I remember to stay calm.
    I ask him, 'How long have you been here?'

HALIM: Not very long. I expected to stay longer, but I'm going back to Pakistan for a little while.

ANNA: 'I thought you were Indian.'

HALIM: No, I'm Canadian. My parents are from Pakistan.

ANNA: Okay. It's awkward. I didn't mean anything by it. But he's looking at me like, like, I don't know, like I'm stupid or something.

HALIM: So, are you interested?

ANNA: 'It's a bit outside my price range.'
    This annoys him, I can tell. He's thinking, 'Why the mmm-mmm-mmm did you waste my time?' or whatever. I'm good at reading people that way.

HALIM: It's priced very aggressively for the market.

ANNA: What does that even mean? Prices can be high, they can be low, but they cannot be aggressive. A price is not an animal.

He hands me his business card – I won't even try to pronounce his name – and I leave, I don't want to be there anymore. I go back to the coffee shop, and I end up chatting online with Rachel and Andrea and Rob. I tell them what happened. I'm upset. Andrea says I should call the police. Rob says that he hasn't done anything illegal – unethical, maybe, but not illegal.

Rachel googles the guy and sends me a link. It's a picture of these guys at some kind of rally, and one guy's on a megaphone. And Rachel asks me if that's the guy, as in, is the guy with the megaphone the real estate agent.

I tell her I'm not sure, because it's not a great picture – taken on a phone, I think – and it's hard to make out the features. I mean, it's the right skin colour and really dark hair and stuff ... But let's be honest, it's not always super easy to tell them apart. Rachel says that he's a trouble-maker in Pakistan. Probably with links to Al-Qaeda. Like, a terrorist. I tell her that he was well-dressed, you know, and didn't have a beard or anything. 'That doesn't matter,' she says, 'In fact that's one way they integrate to infiltrate.'

Andrea and Rob pipe up at this point, and they're both like, yeah, we can't have Al-Qaeda Nazis bullying us around, blah-blah-blah. Well, okay, but let's not exaggerate. Maybe he's just a guy, you know. And Rachel says, 'Yeah, but you can't just let this go. You gotta do something!'

And you know what? She's right. We're talking about my home here. So I'll go talk to him, and maybe, I don't know, maybe I'll get an apology. That would be something.

So you see, the intention was good, right?

Anna pauses, expecting, perhaps, an answer.

Anyway. Andrea says, 'Just be careful,' but no worries – I don't go anywhere without my pepper spray.

So I go back. I know the door code downstairs, and they haven't changed it. Up the elevator, to the door. And I'm about to knock but I listen in and I hear, I hear, um, moaning. Not very loud, but definite moaning. And I remember then that Muslims pray five times a day, and they do it out loud. So I figure that's what he's doing, and that gives me pause. Because you know, I would never want to interrupt someone praying, right? So I wait.

When the moaning stops, I knock.

There's jostling of some kind – is someone else in there? – and I knock again. The door opens and the Indian guy answers, but he looks a little worse for wear. He's tucking in his shirt –

HALIM: It's *you*.

ANNA: 'Yes.'

He just stands there and doesn't move or anything, he's not inviting me in and that makes me suspicious. And there's a smell, a definite smell in the air.

HALIM: What do you want?

ANNA: I'll tell you what – there's no more of that smooth real estate talk now. '

I wanted to tell you that I lived in this apartment before you bought it.'

HALIM: Oh-kay.

ANNA: 'You evicted me. This was my home.'

HALIM: Listen, I don't know what your deal is, I'm really sorry you got evicted and all that, but I own this condo, yeah?

ANNA: 'I understand that, sir,' – I thought the 'sir' was important – 'but you've really put me out.'

HALIM: Uh-huh.

ANNA: 'How do you plan to atone for this?'

HALIM: For fuck's sake –

ANNA: I'm about to answer when he says –

HALIM: I suppose you want money, is that it?

ANNA: Now let's be honest. That is a weird thing to say.
   He puts his hand in his pocket, you know, like he's gonna take out his wallet, but it's not there. So he turns around and walks back in ... and I follow him.

HALIM: Un-fucking-believable.

ANNA: 'Excuse me – '

HALIM: I didn't say you could come in.

ANNA: Well, that's rich!
   He grabs his ... wallet-clip or something, and pulls off three one-hundred-dollar bills.

   This sinks in.

Who carries hundred-dollar bills around? I'm sorry, but that is odd.

HALIM: Here. Go find yourself a hobby, will you?

ANNA: I look at the money –

HALIM: Take the goddamn money and get out of here!

ANNA: 'Please, do not take the Lord's name in vain!'
And he kinda scrunches up his face and –

Halim laughs, an honest-to-God laugh.

It's like I've just told him the funniest joke he's ever heard.
But it's not funny. This is my home we're talking about,
right?
I wait for him to stop laughing.
'Sir, I don't appreciate your mocking. I'm only asking that
you respect my belief in a higher power.'
He waves the money in my face –

HALIM: This *is* the higher power.

ANNA: I wait, I wait for the shame to rise in him, but there's
nothing. There's not the faintest trace of red in his cheeks.
So I can't help but ask myself, 'Is God absent from this
man?'
He tries to give me the money again. To forcibly put it in
my hands. He grabs my arm.
'Stop!'

HALIM: Take the money and get the fuck out of here!

ANNA: I reach into my purse, pull out my pepper spray and point
it at him.

HALIM: Whoa, now, let's calm down.

ANNA: 'I'm perfectly calm. You're the one grabbing me.'

HALIM: I'm sorry. I'm sorry, okay?
Listen, what did I ever do to you? I don't even know you.

ANNA: 'I was evicted because of you.'

HALIM: It's not my fault the owner sold the condo. This whole situation is not my fault.

ANNA: 'All right. Then whose fault is it?'
He looks at me and says – with a straight face, he says this to me with a straight face –

HALIM: Iceland.

ANNA: 'Excuse me?'

HALIM: If you're looking for someone to blame, blame Iceland.

ANNA: 'Shame on you. Shame on you for treating this like a joke.'

HALIM: I'm not treating this –

ANNA: I spray him right in the face –

HALIM: My eyes! Jesus! What the fuck? Argh!

ANNA: He starts to howl like a dog. I must of got 'im good because he starts to heave and wobble and then trips over a purse and falls backwards and there's an awful sound, a cracking sound, as he hits his head on the coffee table.
And the thought that's going through my mind is, 'I saw something like this on *Law & Order*.'

He's lying on the ground. He's not moving.

I'm shaking. It's really weird but I'm 'shaking like a Quaker,' as my mom would say. I kneel by him and I can't get too close, I'm having trouble breathing because of the pepper spray ... but he's still alive, his chest still rises and he's making a wheezing sound. There's also some blood, there's some blood pooling around his head and I don't know what to do.

I pray. I pray and I hope God will hear me and tell me what to do, right?

Show him mercy. Do not let him suffer.

I take one of the pillows from the couch, and I put it over his face. And I sit on the pillow.

I sit on the pillow.

And d'you know what's going through my head?

The question. The same question I want to ask you.

Why did God not tell me to call an ambulance?

KASSANDRA: I decide to call Mattias, but that's when the bathroom door opens –

ANNA: What do you know about Iceland?

KASSANDRA: ' … What?'

ANNA: What do you know about Iceland? It's a country.

KASSANDRA: 'Yes, of course – '

ANNA: Well?

KASSANDRA: 'It's where the volcano erupt.'

ANNA: …

KASSANDRA: 'A few years ago. Planes could not fly?'

ANNA: That's not it.

KASSANDRA: 'In the novel *Brave New World*? It is where people
are sent if they have … independent thought? They're sent to
Iceland, so they live far away from people.'

ANNA: That doesn't make sense.

She shakes her head.

What did he mean? Why would he say that? Why?

KASSANDRA: 'I'm sorry, I do not know.'

The look on the woman's face make me think of expression Memm use. She would say this to me and Jannu when we were disappointed. She says, 'Elu ei ole ainult vikerkaar ega kutsikad.' It means, 'Life is not rainbows and puppy dogs.'

The woman turns to leave and I realize that I must do something if the john is to live.

So I say, 'Please, can you call ambulance?'

ANNA: Don't you dare look at me like that, you dirty fucking whore!

KASSANDRA: She puts a hand over her mouth, and again her cheeks get very red. She opens her bag and takes out – I don't make this up – she takes out a piece of, of soap. She bite it.

She shakes her head.

The woman puts the soap back in her purse and leaves. She doesn't look at me. I expect her to slam the door but she close it quietly behind her.

Now I really do not know what to do.

That's when I hear something, it's a sound like bottle of Coke that is opened very slowly. There is now an odour in the air, a very strong, very bad odour.

I look at the john and I realize what has happen. He has, how you say? His bowels have empty.

He is dead.

She is lost for a moment.

I get dressed and call Mattias. I tell him about the dead john. He stay calm and say, 'It's no problem, I'll send someone.' But when I tell him about the woman, he is agitated. 'You let her leave? Get out of there!' 'But what about fingerprints?' 'They will not matter,' he says, 'if police find you in the apartment!' We argue. Does he not understand that I want to make my life here, that I cannot afford to have my fingerprints in the system? 'I will clean the apartment with bleach,' I say. He yell at me: 'You don't have time!' And he is silent. I can hear him thinking. 'Kassa,' he says finally, 'If you're that worried, burn it.'

She nods to herself.

The cupboards are empty but I find a bottle of vodka. I begin to pour it on the furniture, but I stop when I notice the black grill, to make food, you know, on the balcony. There is a bottle of lighter fluid beside it.

She clears her throat.

I open the lighter fluid, and I, how you say? I spray it on the curtains. On the furniture. On the walls. On – everywhere.

It's middle of afternoon. This is important. It means there will not be many people in the building.

I take the cloth hanging from oven handle, and I, how you say, marinate it? In the vodka. I push it down the neck of the bottle a little bit, so I have something like Molotov cocktail. I light it.

I throw it into the living room. It lands on the corner of coffee table and shatters into many pieces.

I watch as very quickly fire spreads through the apartment. It will not take long.

The sound of a conflagration grows louder.

I leave and go across the street to coffee shop. I sit and watch as smoke comes out and the fire alarm in building goes off.

Flames now come out of the window, and people evacuate from the building and make a crowd in front.

It takes only a few minutes for the fire trucks to arrive, and I think this is a good time to leave. On my way out, I look once more at the apartment, and the smoke and flames are very thick now. It looks like there is a tiny volcano inside the apartment.

There are two young men standing next to me, both dressed in suits. One of them turn to me and says, 'What happened?'

I should not have said anything. I should have just walk away. But how to explain ...? He look like Jannu, this man. Not exactly, of course, but he have the same eyes as him.

Perhaps this is why I suddenly feel urge to scream, to yell at the man. I want to say, 'It's your gambling debt!'

She speaks in Estonian, her voice full of rage.

Mis sul viga on? Kas sa ei näe mida sa teed? Kas sa ei mõista oma tegevuse tagajärgi? Miks sa ei õpi minevikust, miks sa ei saa aru, et me oleme mõttetud loomad? Miks sa ei saa jagada? Miks on võrdõiguslikkus nii hirmuäratav? Ja kuhu me lõpuks jõuame, kui asjad nii edasi lähevad? Mis sul viga on?

She shakes her head.

But instead I swallow these words and I say to him: 'Something to do with Iceland.'

He looks at me like I'm crazy. He and his friend laugh. He says, 'Uh, okay then.'

And I, my throat goes dry, yes? And I put my hand on my chest, like this.

She puts her hand on her chest.

And that's when I feel it.

She pulls out Halim's money clip from her bra.

His money. And I remember now, that I take it before leaving the apartment. That I do it automatically, without thinking.

She looks at the money, then back at the audience.

Why would I ... ?

Kassandra looks at the money clip. She's deciding whether or not to keep the money ...

The sound of a great, raging fire grows stronger and stronger: it feels as if the theatre, the city, the entire world will be consumed by it.

Finally, Kassandra makes a decision. But before we find out what it is –

BLACKOUT.

FAROE ISLANDS

FAROE ISLANDS

Faroe Islands premiered at the Rhubarb Festival on February 22, 2013, with the following artistic team:

Dara: Jessica Moss

Director: Ravi Jain
Stage Manager: Kat Chin

DARA

A meeting room in a community centre. Chairs are set up in a circle. On a table are name tags, pens, cups and a coffee dispenser.

Dara greets the audience as they wander in. She's in her early twenties, affable and obese.

Dara encourages everyone to fill out a name tag, have coffee, and take a seat.

So welcome everyone! I just want to say how delighted I am about the turnout, it's really ... how awesome that you all showed up, I mean, showed up in person and everything, to talk about whale activism!

She puts her hand on her heart.

My name is Dara, and this is officially the first meeting of the Whale Action Hub, or ...

She makes a claw with her hand and makes a breaching motion.

WAH!

She shrugs.

It's like a, a call sign. Or whatever.
   Now I know Whale Action Network probably sounds better, but then the acronym is WAN, and that's no good. Actually, you'd be amazed at how hard it is to find a name for a group that has a good acronym –

She waves her hands frantically.

I'm digressing!

My point is, WAH has a nice ring to it. Just make sure you pronounce the 'W' properly, sometimes it can come out like an 'R' and then it sounds like some kind of vegan-slash-raw-food thing. The image we want to conjure here is more, you know, Chewbacca than uncooked vegetables, am I right?

She makes a claw with her hand and makes a breaching motion.

WAH!

Okay, so, we're gonna have to keep it short today: we were accidentally double-booked with an AA meeting. Which, can I just say?

She points to the Beer Store across the street.

That's a little bit cruel.

Anyways ... I thought I'd start by taking a few minutes to tell you a little bit about my background as an activist, you know, for context, and share how I came to care about whales. Then we'll open up the discussion and find out about *you*, and see what ideas we can come up with about first steps. All good?

She smiles as she takes in the group.

My mother made me an activist. And by that, I don't mean that she was an activist herself, but rather she unwittingly forced me to become one. See, I don't know about you, but high school wasn't exactly the best years of my life ...

She points to her body.

Cruelty is a talent honed during teenagehood, and in Grade 6 Jessica Bouchard baptized me Gee-Gee, which is the shortened form of 'Gobble Gobble.' Apparently, at lunch one day I ate my pb-and-jelly sandwich with an eagerness that rubbed her the wrong way.

She shrugs.

I eat quickly, it's true.

Point being, the nickname stuck throughout high school, along with the frequent and frankly uninspired elephant and whale references. Sometimes they'd mix their metaphors, you know, 'Moby Dick – thar she blows! Gobble gobble!'

Philistines, am I right?

Although now that I think of it, I'm grateful no one was ever motivated enough to actually read *Moby Dick*, because then they'd discover it's a sperm whale, and that would've been a whole other –

She whisks the thought away with her hands.

The other really fat girl in my grade, Becky DeMauer, she never shook off the moniker someone – okay, it was Bryce Fraser – wrote on the blackboard, calling Becky a, quote, 'Husky Titted Cum Dumpster.'

So all things considered, I had it pretty good with Gee-Gee, you know?

I bring this up because at the time, I blamed my mother for being overweight. See, my mother was fine in general, but she had 'rules' we had to follow …

Some made sense, you know, like it was forbidden to go to bed with wet hair or you had to put your hand up before farting. Others weren't so straightforward, like no humming – why *not*? – and then there were the weird ones, like the tv volume always had to be set to an even number or end in five.

But the one rule she believed in with a kind of religious fervour was that we always had to finish our plates. You know that old chestnut, 'Think of the starving children in Africa?' My mother actually said that shit. Out loud. 'Dara, darling, there are thousands of children in Africa who have nothing to eat at all.'

She rolls her eyes.

Adults got it too, albeit in a slightly different form. With my dad, for example, she'd look at his plate and say, 'Barry, please. Ethiopia.' Which is hilarious, because my father has an American sense of geography.

On this one particular Thanksgiving dinner – I must've been twelve or thirteen – my cousin Ashley had smuggled over some of the Halloween candy her mother had bought. They were 'planners,' you know, the kind of family that bought Christmas ornaments in July. Anyway, we ate a *lot* of candy before dinner.

She's a bit of a holy terror, Ashley. When she was three, I was four or five and she said that if she could, she'd put a poopy diaper on a popsicle stick, put it in the freezer, and once it was frozen serve it to me for dessert. It should be no surprise that this is the same kid who discovered the c-word at thirteen and proceeded, every time her mother asked her to do something, to answer, 'I'm sorry, I *cunt* hear you.'

Um, so, anyway, I'd eaten all this candy, and of course, an hour later I'm sitting in front of my half-finished plate of mashed potatoes and turkey and stuffing and I cannot put another forkful of food in my mouth. And I think that maybe, maybe my mother won't notice, you know? I catch my dad's eye and he looks at me and it takes a second but he gets what's going on. And he does that thing, you know, when he angles his head a bit, like this, and gives me the universal 'Suck it up, Charlie' look.

And Ashley, wonderful little Ashley who somehow found room for everything on *her* plate, she sees this and probably figures out what is going on, you know? And she says to my dad,

'Do you want some more?' which pulls my mother out of her conversation with Uncle Lou and puts Dad and I back on her gastro-dar.

'Barry?' she says.

And my dad looks at her and says, 'I'm good, thanks.'

My mom starts to turn back to Uncle Lou and maybe maybe maybe but ... NO! She glances over at me –

She raises her fists in frustration.

'Dara, finish your plate please.'

Let me be very clear here: when I say I was full, I don't mean in a nice, satisfied kind of way. Those last few forkfuls you take, you know, not entirely sure if you'll get them down? Yeah. Already had those. We were at the point where I knew, with absolute certainty, that if I ate another fucking crumb, I was going to go *Meaning of Life* on everyone ...

She mimes puking.

So I say, 'I'm not hungry anymore.'

And a hush falls over the table.

'Darling, there are starving children in Africa who don't have the luck you do. So please finish your plate.'

I look at my plate. My father tries to intervene –

'Maggie – '

But she puts up her finger, you know, effectively telling him to back the fuck off.

So my father backs the fuck off. I'm on my own.

My mother glares at me, you know, *waiting.*

And then I remember the look she'd given me earlier that day as she helped me put on a dress. I don't think she meant for me to see it, but she did the lifted-eyebrow-and-slight-shake-of-the-head thing as I tried to squeeze the dress past my waist. But I saw it. And it made me feel like shit, frankly.

And now I was expected to finish my plate?

Okay.

I push my chair back from the table, and I get up.

'Dara ... ' she says.

'I will be right back,' I say as politely as I can.

And I go off to my dad's office – he's an accountant and works from home and also runs an eBay business selling vintage Star Wars toys – and I take a padded envelope and write on it with a Sharpie before heading back to the dining room. Everyone stops talking when they see me come back, you know, pretending like nothing is wrong or whatever.

I take the plate and dump my food into the envelope.

And this takes a few moments, because I wait for the mashed potatoes to inch. Their. Way. Down.

I put the plate back on the table, and I seal the envelope. I walk over to my mother, who is as white as a sheet.

I plop the envelope in front of her. She looks down at it: 'From: Pearson Family, Canada. To: Starving Children, Africa.' My mother looks at the envelope, then looks up at me, gobsmacked.

And I don't know what possesses me – I guess I was, like, really really angry – but I look my mom right in the eyes and I say, 'You should probably send it express. Margaret.'

(I *never* call my mom Margaret.)

Her mouth falls open a little bit, you know, like she's going to say something, but nothing comes out. Instead, she looks over at my dad, who immediately gets up and grabs me by the arm and drags me to my room.

I'm bawling, of course, wondering how many decades I'm going to be grounded for.

And my father pulls me into my room and shuts the door. It takes me a second to realize that he's not gone, I mean, that he didn't just leave me there.

Instead, he kneels down in front of me and pulls me into a hug. You gotta understand, my dad isn't the touchy-feely type. But he's just holding me, he's squeezing me tight and I'm so shocked that I stop crying and I don't know how to react, and then he pulls away and smiles. He smiles and looks at me and – it's funny, I remember this so vividly – he brushes a strand of hair from my face and says, 'Honey, I am so proud of you.'

My mother never told me to finish my plate again.

I was also grounded for two months.

Meh. It was worth it.

Because that day, I learned that I could change things. *We* can change things.

She laughs.

I'm so sorry, I didn't mean for that to be so ... convoluted! I'm such a dork. I told you about my digressions, right?

She waves her hands.

The whales!

Now, you may think I became Little Miss Activism after that, but truthfully? Not so much. The irony of being fat is that you're also invisible, in a way, and I was perfectly comfortable with that.

Until I met Rachel.

She smiles.

I was at university at this point, at York, doing English – I loved reading and I thought I'd like to teach. And also, my grades weren't good enough for U of T.

It was a cold March day, and I was leaving the Scott Library after studying for exams when I saw this petite blonde woman handing out pamphlets, you know, and there was a big sign behind her of a poor whale on its side, its stomach cut open, and above it the words 'MURDER' with an exclamation mark. And she was chanting 'Stop the Whale Murder!'

Look. Sure it's old school, but that's a pretty ballsy thing to do in front of a library. During exams.

Anyway, I was staring because I had a thought, and I guess Rachel noticed me and she said, 'Do you know anything about the grindadráp?' And I'm like, 'The what?' and she says, 'The whale hunt in the Faroe Islands. Do you know what they do?' And I shake my head.

And she proceeds to describe, in the most inarticulate way possible, how it happens. Seriously, it was the kind of explanation where you have to stop the person every minute to figure out who's doing what. Clearly, she was passionate about the issue, but ...

She shrugs.

For those who've never seen it, picture a bay, and there's a pod of about, I dunno, thirty or forty pilot whales swimming towards the shore, you know, like this –

She mimes breaching whales with her hand.

(FYI, they babysit each other's calves.)

And they're being chased by, like, a hundred boats. As they get close to shore, there's a sudden rush of people, a kind of tidal wave of people, that run towards the whales. And when they reach the whales, they *club* them to death. You can see the whales panicking, either because they're being clubbed or because they're *watching* others being clubbed. By the time it's finished, the water, the ocean water, is *red* with blood. It's *horrifying*.

Anyway, her description of it was ten times as long and half as sensical. But you know what? This was near the end of my first year at York, and so far university was a giant disappointment. I mean, you spend your entire teenage years thinking of and being indoctrinated about the importance of going to university, you know, how higher education is really important and yadda, yadda, yadda ...

With her hand, she mimes her mother going on and on about it.

Right? So expectations are high. Anyway, I expected to arrive at York and find people who were motivated and excited and smart and instead there was a lot of confused, angry, lazy people who weren't interested in learning. They're interested in getting good marks, they're interested in being told what to do, they're being taught *what* to think about things, not *how*. It's fucking depressing. So when I'm faced with a girl handing me a pamphlet, who is trying to actually *do* something to make a difference ...

She shrugs.

I told her I'd help.

I pointed to her sign. 'Nix the exclamation mark,' I said. She frowned. 'It undermines your argument. It's more ominous, more threatening if the word 'murder' appears without punctuation.'

I guess you can say that's how we became friends or whatever.

So pretty soon I'm handing out pamphlets with her, you know, and it's kind of amazing how soul-crushing an experience that is. Listen, I know what it's like to feel invisible, and this made me feel worse. Person after person after person ignores you, and by ignoring, I mean they pretend like you don't exist, like they can't hear or see you.

The amazing thing, to me, is that this doesn't faze Rachel. It's like she's a superhero.

I got a full demonstration of her powers on the day this douchebag stopped to talk to us, you know, and he's got his two fratarded buddies with him. When I explain to him that we're doing this to stop the whale hunt, he says, 'Are you feeling endangered?' which I guess was his way of saying how much he misses being in high school or something ... I do what I normally do in such circumstances, which is basically express my contempt and disdain for such comments via a glare.

Rachel, however, takes a different approach. She steps in between me and the douche, and asks him, 'What did you say to my friend?' It's a challenge, and we all know it. So the douche shrugs and says, 'Whatever.' I figure that's the end of it, but Rachel echoes his, 'Whatever?' and then she ... Do you know what she does?

She smiles.

She starts to cry. And you can tell the three douches are at a complete loss; one of them asks, 'Hey, you okay?' Rachel shakes her head and the cries turn to loud, gasping sobs. The douches look at me, and I just shrug. I mean, I've no idea ...

She shrugs, then smiles.

Guess what happens when a girl – a cute, blond, five-foot-nothing girl – standing by the entrance of a busy library, surrounded by three fridge-sized dudes, starts to sob uncontrollably?

People stop. And stare. And a couple of people, both guys and girls, come over. And they ask, 'What's going on?' And herein lies Rachel's genius: she doesn't answer, she just *points* to the douchebag. And *everybody* turns to look at him.

'I, uh, I was just, um, making a joke, and then, she just –'

The best part – apart from *campus security* showing up – was seeing the expression on his face when Rachel pointed at him. Because even with his limited intellect, he understood right away he was toast. *Nothing* he could say was getting him out of this one.

By the end of it, even one of his buddies was shaking his head at him, you know, in silent acknowledgment that his friend had crossed a line.

It. Was. Awesome.

Gandhi had hunger strikes. MLK had marches. Rachel had tears and she wasn't afraid to use them.

Anyway, that night we watched *The Cove* at her place for like the *n*th time, and as usual it got Rachel riled up about the Faroes ...

So I said, 'Let's *go* there.'

Rachel turned to me and nodded: 'Fuck yeah.'

And that evening, only slightly inebriated, we brainstormed a two-pronged plan of attack: one, deliver a petition to the Faroese prime minister, and two, shoot the grindadráp and make a documentary to upload on YouTube. The doc is Rachel's idea, she's super-stoked about it, she's like –

She makes a 'frame' with her hands.

'We'll shoot from a boat, you know, going towards the shore, where we can see the mob waiting for us ... '

'I say, "Us?"'

'Yeah, because *we're the whales*. I mean it's the POV of the whales but it's also us ... think of it like *The Cove* meets the opening sequence of *Saving Private Ryan*. I mean, it's gonna blow people's brains, Dara.'

We revamp our Facebook group, we put up a kick-ass website, we start an online petition and we even email the Faroese PM. And by 'we,' I mean 'me.'

I don't mean to be bitchy, but Rachel's skill set doesn't include organization. Which is fine, I'm happy to do it because, well, it's important. And all that.

At first, honestly, the response is pretty underwhelming. I mean, our Facebook group stagnates at about two hundred people; our petition is doing a little better, we're just shy of a thousand signatures ... But these aren't exactly 'tipping point' numbers, you know?

So we meet with – I think this is right – Rachel's cousin's girlfriend's mother ...

She makes air quotation marks.

'Eleanor.'

She's a marketing VP at an ad agency or something.

Anyway, so she meets with us and looks at our online stuff and says it's all well-written and everything, but that we don't have a 'face for the campaign.' Rachel says that's what the whales are, but Eleanor shakes her head and says, 'The whales aren't the ones delivering a petition to the Prime Minister. I imagine one of you ... ?'

Neither of us had thought about that, I guess because we'd always assumed we'd do it together.

I ask, 'Can there be two faces?'

And Eleanor does this amazing thing where she shakes her head and says, 'Sure' at the same time.

'Is it better if it's just one?' says Rachel.

Eleanor shrugs and says, 'Yes. Much better.'

Rachel and I look at each other. We both know, of course, but neither one of us wants to say it.

'I'm so bad with words,' Rachel says.

'Oh, that's fine,' says Eleanor. 'Just have Dara come up with a few talking points, and stick to those.'

And just like that, Rachel became the public face of End the Whale Hunt Now, exclamation mark.

Which, for the record, has a stupid acronym.

She shrugs.

The thing is, it worked.

Eleanor put us in touch with a journalist at the *Globe and Mail*, and we got an article – with a photo of Rachel floating on a plastic dolphin in a pool – that pushed our campaign into a whole other sphere. Other papers called, and Rachel was invited to speak on a couple of morning shows.

On the same day we got our hundred thousandth signature, we got an email from Páll Jacobsen, who works for the Faroe Ministry of Fisheries. He's been asked to liaise with us for our visit, and to answer any questions we may have about the grindadráp.

And I remember when I called Rachel over to my laptop to show her the email, she read it and then came right up to the screen, you know, and inhaled ...

She demonstrates the inhale.

And she said, 'Do you smell that?' I scowled, you know, like, WTF? And she smiled and said, 'That's what fears smells like. We have twice as many signatures as they have people.'

That's the same night I noticed – this is gonna sound really weird, I know – but I went to the washroom and noticed that she'd tossed an empty toilet paper roll in the *garbage*.

She shrugs.

At the time I didn't think anything of it ... But now? I wonder if it was a sign.

With the signatures continuing to add up, it was time to book our flights and make it official. I don't think it'll come as a surprise that getting to the Faroes is not cheap, but I don't think either one of us thought it would be as expensive as it turned out to be. And because of all the time I'd spent on the campaign, I'd quit my weekend job at Second Cup and flunked out of my Chaucer class, which meant I'd have to pay for another class.

To be honest, it was probably for the best. It meant I could hold down the fort while Rachel was in the Faroes. We'd found her a relatively cheap hostel in Tórshavn, although we'd been warned that food was going to be expensive. Incredibly, Páll

Jacobsen had been very helpful in arranging a lot of this stuff. Rachel knew they were just trying to soften us up. 'We're up to 115,000. They're shaking in their boots!'

I smiled and hoped that the Faroes were ready for Hurricane Rachel.

A week before departure, we printed our petition for the PM. We had 122,000 signatures, and we could squeeze 175 on each page in a ten-point font, double-sided. It came to just about 350 pages total and we neatly bound it with screws.

When I held it in my hands – the weight of it? Knowing what it represented? I think it was the proudest moment of my life. Isn't that silly?

She fidgets with her hands.

Rachel left on a Tuesday, and her carry-on luggage consisted of her camera gear and our petition. I hugged her goodbye and she said, 'You don't give bear hugs, you give whale hugs!'

She shrugs.

(I wasn't quite sure how to take that.)

And for the first week she was there, we emailed every day and I'd update the website with photos and blog posts of her adventures. She'd met with Páll Jacobsen, and was now working out a time to meet with the PM to give him the petition.

And then the emails stopped. Not all of a sudden or anything, but I started to get short responses to long questions. This was around the time the grindadráp was supposed to start, so I figured maybe she was out shooting ... but it was strange. It was strange to be in daily contact with someone and then not.

Finally, I sent her an email asking for an update on the petition and for footage of the grindadráp to post on the website. She responded with: 'Let's Skype tomorrow 10 a.m. your time.'

She smiles.

Cue ominous music!

So the next morning we finally get to speak, sort of face-to-face, I guess. She looks a little tired, but otherwise the same. We chit-chat for a few minutes, she asks me about things in Toronto and Che, her betta fish. And there's an edge to her voice, you know?

And I realize that she's nervous. *Rachel* is nervous.

'What's going on?' I ask.

She shrugs, and then says, 'Nothing, why?'

'Did you get any footage of the grindadráp?'

Rachel shakes her head and says, 'Not yet.' She looks away and then adds, 'But I delivered the petition!'

'To the Prime Minister?'

She nods.

'What did he say?'

'Who?'

'The Prime Minister!'

'Oh. He said thank you.'

'That's *it*?'

Rachel shrugs. 'Apparently they get them all the time.'

'And what did he say when you asked him to respond within the week?'

And here Rachel twitches her nose, you know, like this ...

She twitches her nose.

And says, 'Oh. I forgot to ask him that.'

Seriously. Who is this empty, vapid cow I'm Skyping with?

'What the hell, Rach?'

'Look,' she says, 'Things here aren't exactly what we thought, you know? I mean, the pilot whale drive is pretty dramatic, of course, but Dara – they use the whales for food, okay? It's not like they're killing them for sport. And they showed me how they do it, it's actually the most efficient and humane way to kill them, under the circumstances.'

She leans forward on her chair.

'Under the circumstances?'

She kept going, something about how abundant pilot whales are, I think, but at this point I'm so shell-shocked I'm just staring at the screen ...

That's when I notice her surroundings. It's a really nice place, a little messy but definitely homey.

'Where are you?' I ask.

'What do you mean? I'm in the Faroes –'

'No, I mean right now? You're not at the hostel.'

And I can see Rachel is suddenly caught off-guard.

'Oh yeah, no, I'm over at someone's. It's ... '

And Rachel bites her lip and looks off to the side, and waves someone over.

This guy enters the frame, and he's – okay, fine, he's very handsome, he's quite, quite beautiful, actually, and he waves over at me with a kind of familiarity that annoys the fuck out of me.

'Hullo!' he says.

'Hi.'

'Dara, this is Páll Jacobsen. Remember him? He works for the Fiskimálará – ' blah-blah-blah or whatever.

'It is so nice to finally meet you!' he says.

And I burst out laughing. Like crazy laughing, you know?

Rachel quickly shoos Páll Jacobsen away.

'Dara, what's wrong? What's the matter? Aren't you happy for me?'

Oh my God – she thinks I'm crying!

And that just sets me off more, you know? I mean – Páll Jacobsen?

She guffaws.

And Rachel's like, 'Please, say something ... '
But the only thing I think to say is ...
I say, 'You're just another moral relativist.'
Then I add, 'And a bitch.'

She shakes her head.

I mean – she can't even recycle *toilet paper rolls*, right?

She puts up her finger.

And then you know what she says? She says –

There's a loud knock at the door.
Dara checks the time.

That's AA, I guess we're ...

She laughs.

Right, right, right! Then she says, 'For God's sake, Dara.
They're just whales.'
That's what she says to me!
'They're just whales!'

There's another loud knock at the door.

OH-KAY!

She turns back to the group.

In a harsh, aggressive tone.

Whales are people too!

Registers what she's just said.

A sharp knock at the door.

Of course, we – we've got to go. I'm sorry we ran out of time ...'I hope you'll come back ... next week ... thank you ... uh ...

Dara, in a daze, can't find the words to continue.

BLACKOUT.

ACKNOWLEDGMENTS

My thanks to the following individuals and companies:

Dr. Garry Clarke, Emeritus Professor of Geophysics at the University of British Columbia, for sharing his knowledge and experience of glaciology.

Dr. Rob Brander, Senior Lecturer at the University of New South Wales, for his help with rip currents.

Heili Orav, Virve Aljas, and Killi Mirka for their help with the Estonian in *Iceland*.

Michael Rubenfeld and the team at the SummerWorks Theatre Festival.

Laura Nanni and the team at the Rhubarb Festival.

Dustin Olson and Esther Barlow and the team at The Bridge Theatre Company.

My agent, Pam Winter, and the team at the Gary Goddard Agency.

My first readers, including Johanne Archambault, Pierre Billon, Jenny Earle, Michele Mani, and Aislinn Rose.

My editors, Alana Wilcox and Leigh Nash, along with Evan Munday and Heidi Waechtler at Coach House Books.

And finally, my deepest gratitude to the artists listed in the production credits; their insight, feedback and suggestions have made the plays all the better.

ABOUT THE AUTHOR

Nicolas Billon grew up in Ottawa, Paris and Montreal. His vocation as a writer first surfaced around the age of six, when he wrote stories on index cards, which he stapled together and sold to his mother for a tidy profit. Since then, his plays and translations have been produced at the Stratford Festival, Soulpepper Theatre, Canadian Stage and the Théâtre d'Aujourd-d'hui. Nicolas also writes for film.

Typeset in Ronaldson, the very first American metal typeface, which was designed by Alexander Kay in 1884, for the Mackeller, Smiths & Jordan type foundry of Philadelphia, and was lost to time until it was digitized in 2006 by Patrick Griffin of Canada Type.

Printed at the old Coach House on bpNichol Lane in Toronto, Ontario, on Zephyr Antique Laid paper, which was manufactured, acid-free, in Saint-Jérôme, Quebec, from second-growth forests. This book was printed with vegetable-based ink on a 1965 Heidelberg kord offset litho press. Its pages were folded on a Baumfolder, gathered by hand, bound on a Sulby Auto-Minabinda and trimmed on a Polar single-knife cutter.

Edited for the press by Leigh Nash and Alana Wilcox
Designed by Leigh Nash
Photo of Nicolas Billon by Trish Lindström
Cover illustration by Jonathan Bartlett, www.bartlettstudio.com

Coach House Books
80 bpNichol Lane
Toronto ON M5S 3J4
Canada

416 979 2217
800 367 6360

mail@chbooks.com
www.chbooks.com